OJO DE DIOS · EYE OF GOD

OJO DE DIOS ◆ EYE OF GOD
BY CHARLET ALBAUM

Published in association with
Parade Magazine

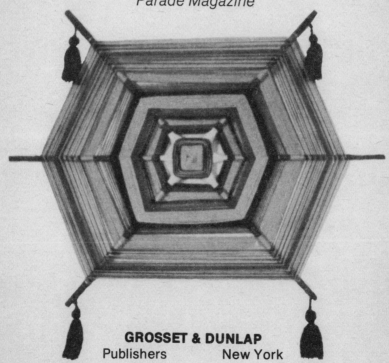

GROSSET & DUNLAP
Publishers   New York

Contents

OJO DE DIOS · EYE OF GOD

Ojo de Dios

What is an Ojo de Dios?

Any Southwesterner can tell you. Borrowed from ancient traditions of the nearby Pueblo and Mexican Indians, the Ojo de Dios (Spanish for Eye of God) is a colorful, authentic talisman, said to bring good luck, good fortune and favor from the gods.

The Ojo de Dios (pronounced *o-ho day dee-os*) is crafted by weaving various colored yarns onto sticks. The many lovely shapes and designs that can be made easily and quickly, to decorate as well as protect the home, have turned this little-known Indian folk art into one of the Southwest's most popular creative art forms. And the handicraft is fast being discovered by other sections of the country. Easily mastered by young and old alike, Ojo-making offers excellent opportunity for creative expression, relaxation and personal satisfaction, at extremely low cost.

The more simple Ojo is made of two pieces of crossed wood upon which various colors of yarn are wrapped to form a diamond pattern flowing outward from the center or "eye" of the construction. It can be made with the front side smooth and the back side revealing the crossed sticks; or it may be double-woven so that both sides are smooth rendering the Ojo equally presentable front and back. After a little practice, Ojos may also be fashioned in a variety of geometric shapes.

Indian craftsmen throughout the years have indicated the importance of the eye of the design in a number of ways—sometimes by leaving it unwrapped, sometimes by using black yarn to represent the pupil, or by attaching a mirror to enable the Eye of God to see better. The yarn and wood figure, then, symbolizes contact with the unknown, and serves as a means of communication between man and the god or goddess it was woven to represent.

Origin

The story of the Ojo's origins is a fascinating one. Archaeologists have discovered the sacred objects on widely separated Indian sites. In dry graves of the Ancon Necropolis of Peru, God's Eyes were found among mummy bundles and in baskets containing weaving tools and spindle whorls. They were also fashioned into headdresses of false mummy heads and, in one instance, used in place of eyes.

Thousands of miles north, in an ancient Arizonan cliff dwelling, a yucca leaf was found strung around two crossed pieces of wood forming a primitive God's Eye figure.

2

Today, in the United States, the making of Ojos is still a part of the art and tradition of the Pimas, some of the Pueblo people, and some Navahos who weave a figure similar to the God's Eye called an Owl Bugaboo which is used to subdue unruly children. The Pueblos often use Ojos as hair ornaments.

The Eye of God is also found among the tribal arts of four different Indian peoples of the Sierra Madre country of Northwestern Mexico—the Huichols, the Coras, the Tepehuanes, and the Tarahumaras. The sole example reported from the last tribe was an Ojo hung by a string from the center of a stick and waved back and forth to ward off disease and evil spirits.

Huichol Prayer

The greatest concentration of God's Eyes is found among the Huichol Indians, commonly called the "Happy People." To this tribe, the God's Eye is a symbol of the power of the unknown, to which the figure gives them access. When the Huichol wants a special favor, he will ask the shaman or holy man to construct a God's Eye to represent a certain god of the tribe's pantheon. As the shaman weaves, the suppliant, seated beside him, joins in the prayer. What the suppliant asks is that the Eye of God, being symbolically represented in yarn and wood, seek him out and rest on him.

Completed, the Ojo (which can be compared to an altar) is placed in a temple or other sacred spot reserved for the god being addressed. The colors used in the design vary with the deity: blue or turquoise might represent the Rain god; green, the god of Fertility; and yellow, the Sun god. The Huichol may pray for good health, help in weaving and other crafts, and agricultural success; in short, for anything that will bring him a happy and meaningful life.

The Huichol people call their Ojos *Tsikuli*, their name for the male squash blossom. It is also the name of the mythical first Huichol child. The wool-like substance in the calyx of the blossom probably led to the identification of it with the God's Eye. During the great feast of the green squash blossom, held each October in the Huichol villages, Ojos are prominently displayed. This harvest ceremony or fertility rite is held in honor of Mother East-Water, a goddess identified as the creator of squashes and mother-protector of children. During the fiesta, the hair of the children is banded with Ojos. Ojos are also planted in the squash fields, a demonstration of their importance to the Huichol life scheme.

Kauyuma'li, a son of Mother East-Water, is said to have used the God's Eye in the completion of his task, the making of the earth. Clearly, the Ojo is an important part of a rich tapestry of Indian lore and legend.

We may feel something of the splendor and mystery of the Indian concept of creation represented by an Ojo as it is expressed here by the Uitoto people of Colombia:

> Nothing existed, not even a stick to support the vision; our Father attached the illusion to the thread of a dream and kept it by the aid of his breath. He sounded to reach the bottom of the appearances, because there was nothing. Nothing existed indeed.

> Then the Father again investigated the bottom of the mystery. He tied the empty illusion to the dream thread and pressed the magical substances upon it. Thus by the aid of the dream he held it like a wisp of raw cotton.

While the mystery of the origin of the God's Eye will probably never be fully revealed, we may feel free to enjoy the essential simplicity, purity and beauty of Ojos by reproducing them in forms that suit our own lives. As one Southwestern wit recently put it, "Better the Eye of God than the Eye of the Devil."

Modern Craft

Since the Ojo de Dios symbolizes the desire for good fortune, good health and long life, it is a good emblem to display in your home or to give as a gift. The Eye of God may serve as a wall hanging in homes, offices and even schools, but it looks especially warm and inviting in a den or family room, set against wood paneling or hung above a fireplace. Since it is often made to order, it can enhance any color scheme and be made to fit any space, large or small. The Ojo de Dios offers an inexpensive, handcrafted alternative to the usual store-bought prints of the great masters, mass-produced commercial plaques and pop posters.

Depending on its size, there are literally dozens of ways to display a God's Eye. A single large Ojo on a wall can alter the entire appearance of a room, creating a finishing focal point of color. A giant double-woven (reversible) Ojo, or a number of large Ojos alternating side-by-side, make a lovely, inexpensive room divider. Mounted in a bathroom window, a single Ojo may serve as a colorful shade, allowing sunlight to filter through the weave and cast patterns on the opposite wall. To decorate a patio or as a charm for an outdoor garden, use waterproof, rust-proof rods, and nylon or plastic twine, thus creating a long-lasting, all-weather God's Eye.

Small Ojos, made from ice cream sticks or sugar stirrers, may be double-woven to match the colors in a dining room or kitchen and set in a wooden base as a center-piece. For a colorful and useful desk accessory, mount twin Ojos on a fountain pen stand, or attach them to a set of teak bookends.

At Christmas time, a triangular Ojo made with green yarn and gold cord makes a festive holiday mantlepiece, while smaller Ojos of various colors and designs may be used to decorate the tree. Two coat hangers, thin wire or string, and five or six double-woven Ojos of various sizes can, with a little ingenuity, be turned into a lovely, eye-catching mobile for any time of the year.

A mini-Ojo, made from very fine crochet thread or sport or fingering yarn and woven on a skeleton of match-sticks or toothpicks, is a perfect good luck charm. It may be hung from the rearview mirror of your car, attached to a pocketbook, belt or key chain, or stitched to a piece of rawhide or a comb to serve as a hair ornament. Tiny, deli-cate Ojo earrings with a matching Ojo pendent necklace make an impressive and touching handmade gift for that special friend.

With just a bit of practice, you will soon find yourself creating your own original, two- and three-dimensional de-signs and experimenting with them to serve almost any decorative need.

Large or small, most of the God's Eye projects in this book can be completed alone, in your own home, in a sin-gle day—many in just a few enjoyable hours. However, there are groups such as Senior Citizens, Scouts, women's clubs, and various student societies who have found Ojo parties to be not only stimulating, satisfying and fun but also profitable, bringing needed funds from sales at club, church and charity bazaars.

The Basic Ojo

When constructed entirely with the basic wrap, the Eye of God will look smooth in front and one-dimensional. By using a variety of colored yarns, however, many different effects can be achieved even in this one-dimensional form. Most Ojo craftsmen employ a variety of weaving methods, all variations of the basic front wrap. The changes in the appearance of the figure come about by changing the direction or number of wraps, allowing for open spaces, or simply by varying the size and shape of the sticks used as the skeleton. After learning the basic technique of wrapping the Ojo sticks to make a simple design, learning the variations will come easily. Ojo-making is simple to learn, and mistakes are really unimportant since whatever is "woven" can be easily and quickly undone.

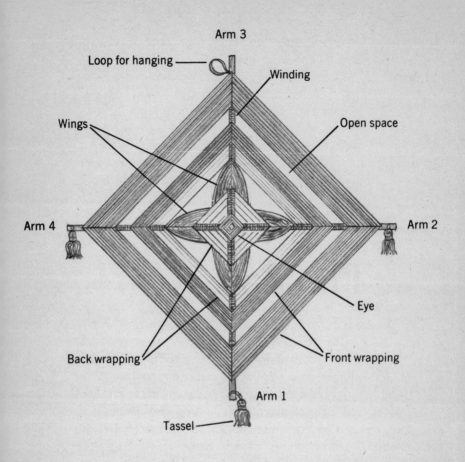

Arm 3

Loop for hanging

Winding

Wings

Open space

Arm 4

Arm 2

Eye

Back wrapping

Front wrapping

Arm 1

Tassel

THE BASIC OJO

Craft Terms

Dowel   Term used in lumberyards and stores for the sticks needed to make the Ojo skeleton.

Skeleton   The entire frame on which the yarn is

wrapped, after the sticks have been measured, cut, notched and glued.

Arm   A spoke formed by the crossed sticks making a skeleton. (The basic Ojo, made with two crossed sticks, has four arms.) For our purposes, throughout this book, the arms are numbered counterclockwise starting at the bottom.

Eye   The junction of the arms, usually covered with the initial yarn wrappings. A mirror, piece of felt or fabric, or other such material may also decorate the eye.

Wrap   Winding the yarn around an arm of the skeleton one complete time, also called a front wrap. The hitch may also be counted as a wrap.

Back wrap   A wrap worked around an arm on the back of the skeleton.

Wing   A special V-shaped design formed by wrapping opposite arms.

Wing wrap   A wrap worked around opposite arms of a skeleton.

Wrap 2, 3, 4, etc.   Wrapping the yarn two, three, four, etc., complete times around the same arm. Used to separate the strands of yarn and prevent bunching, to even off a slightly short arm due to tighter wrappings, and to spread weave to give Ojo a different shape.

Wind   Placing a large number of wrappings (winding yarn) on an arm. Used to cover exposed wood, introduce open areas in the weave, and form various geometrical designs.

Round   A wrap worked counterclockwise around the arms of the skeleton. For certain designs, arms to be wrapped in a round will be so designated, as well as number of wraps each arm should receive per round.

Hitch   A knot (half hitch or clove hitch) used to start and stop the use of various yarn colors and, within colors, to prevent the loosening of the weave. It is often used in conjunction with glue for extra protection.

Weave   The area of yarn stretched between the arms.

Twirling   Rotating the Ojo between the fingertips to facilitate wrapping.

Craft Needs

The necessary equipment and materials needed for Ojo-making are minimal, easily available and quite inexpensive. To construct an 18″ x 18″ basic Ojo, for instance, you should have:

Two 18″ sticks or dowels (36″ dowels are available in most lumber stores) to form a skeleton

Three to six colors of four-ply yarn (1 oz. of each color is usually sufficient) for weaving

A ruler or tape measure to check for needed adjustments in weaving.

A small hand saw and jackknife or chisel and mallet to cut and notch the sticks to be used for the skeleton

White glue to make the skeleton and secure important wrappings

Scissors to cut yarn

You might also find uses for additional craft materials, such as: sandpaper to smooth the rough ends of sticks; paint or stain if you prefer unwrapped sticks to show; and fluffy feathers, cotton balls, beads, leather lacings, gemstones, fabric, etc., to decorate the Ojo. These materials, however, and many others which may also be used creatively in Ojo-crafting, are optional.

Sticks and Dowels

Round sticks to form the skeleton for the Eye of God can be purchased from lumberyards or hardware stores. Usually called dowels, they are often precut to 36″ in length and can be easily cut in half to make a basic 18″ Ojo, or left as is to make a large design. Of course, they may also be cut to any size to fit your needs or plans. Always remember, however, to select a diameter size to match the size of the Ojo. For a large Eye, use dowels ⅜″ or ½″ in diameter. If the dowels are not thick enough for the overall size of the construction, they will bend during the weaving.

Flat or square sticks are often used to create a different look, a different Ojo. These can be purchased precut at a hardware store or they can be cut to order at a lumber store. Prefinished lathe strips, bamboo sticks, curtain rods and dowels are excellent choices.

For small or mini-Ojos, ordinary household objects can be found. Flat toothpicks, ice cream sticks, sugar stirrers and food skewers are quite usable. Even pick-up sticks and tinker toys can be used to make the more delicate designs.

PREPARING THE SKELETON

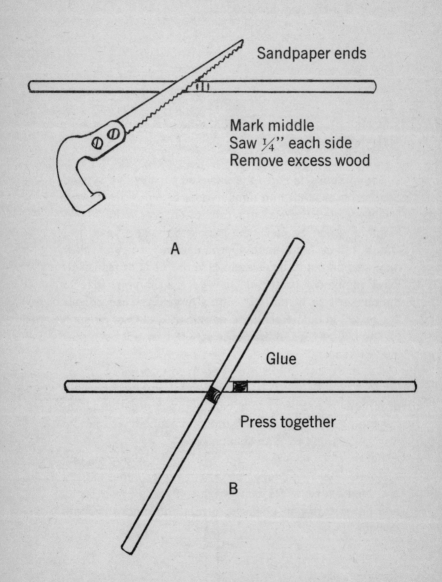

Sandpaper ends

Mark middle
Saw ¼" each side
Remove excess wood

A

Glue

Press together

B

Skeleton

After measuring the sticks or dowels, cutting them to the length desired, and smoothing the ends, notch the center point of each stick as shown. For the 18″ basic Ojo, the notch should be about ½″ wide and should be deep enough to allow the two crossed sticks to fit together snugly, forming a perfect cross. Then glue and press the sticks together at the notch. Wait until the glue is completely dry before you start to make your Ojo de Dios.

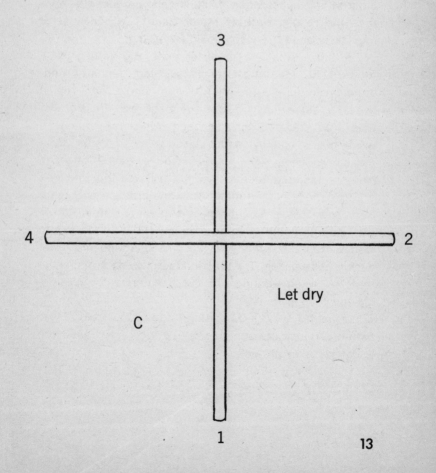

3

4   2

Let dry

C

1

Yarn

Four-ply yarn, traditionally used for making God's Eyes, can be purchased in a great variety of colors. Worsted wool is best, but Orlon gives satisfactory results while offering a few additional shades. Some yarn shops sell a multi-strand yarn which creates a completely different Ojo look. Four or five single-ply strands are gathered together to form a single multi-strand. These gathered strands separate somewhat when strung, allowing you to control their appearance. Multi-strand yarn loosens more than the regular four-ply strand (see TENSION), so it must be wrapped very tightly while weaving.

For those who like to experiment, rug yarn gives a rough, bulky look and is especially good for large constructions. Various colored twines, cords and ropes, available since the popularity of macramé, are also usable. You may, however, choose freely from butcher's twine, mason line, nylon and plastic twine. Since the earliest known Ojos were made of yucca leaves, Mexican ixtle creates an authentically ancient flavor Ojo. The look of these modern craft materials won't produce altogether traditional creations, but they are much too promising to be ignored. Twine or cord may be stiff or awkward to weave around the skeleton, so their use presents fewer design possibilities. Try to use dowels which are small in diameter when working with bulky materials for interesting and unusual results.

For an 18˝ to 24˝ Ojo, using three or four colors, less than one ounce of each color of yarn is usually adequate to complete the project.

Using Color

Color combinations are as limitless as individual taste, but the following suggestions may be helpful:

1. Make one color dominate the overall design.
2. Use at least three colors, preferably four to six.
3. Contrast colors such as black and white, red and green, brown and gold or deep blue and lime.
4. Use three or four shades of the same color gradually going from light to dark or from dark to light.
5. Combine a multicolor yarn with the other colors it contains.
6. Use a light shade against a dark shade—light yellow with gold, orange with red or lavender with purple.
7. Blend colors which go well together—brown, gold, tan and rust.
8. Use like colors together—"earth" colors, bright colors, pastels.

Weaving
the Basic Ojo

After preparing your skeleton (usually in the form of a square cross), you are ready to begin weaving the eye of the God's Eye figure. The first step is to make an appropriate knot to hold the yarn securely in place.

Starting Hitch

The half hitch and the clove hitch (which consists of two half hitches), are quite satisfactory starting knots as they are smooth, flat and easy to make while holding the skeleton. The clove hitch is used to begin wrapping the Ojo and at the beginning and end of each change of yarn, while the half hitch is primarily used at stress points to hold the yarn in place and to keep the weave from relaxing.

To make the half hitch, loop the yarn so that the loose end goes under the strand connected to the skein, as shown.

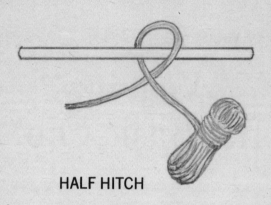

HALF HITCH

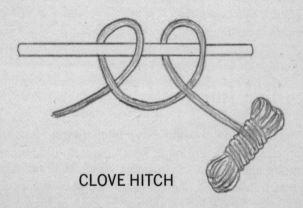

CLOVE HITCH

During wrapping, the half hitch can be made quickly and easily by looping the yarn around the finger of your right hand and slipping the loop onto the end of the arm—like casting on in knitting. Here again, the clove hitch is simply two half hitches so the clove hitch may be done in the same way.

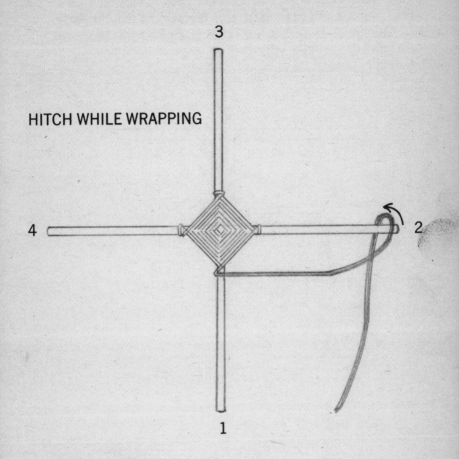

HITCH WHILE WRAPPING

3

4

2

1

Basic Wrap

With the skeleton assembled, and the yarns to be used at hand, you are ready to begin weaving. First, make the starting clove hitch on Arm 1. Tighten the knot, wrap the yarn around the loose end once or twice to hold it down and out of the way and push the knot toward the center. Hold the skeleton in your left hand, thumb in the center front, other fingers in the center back. With the skein of

THE BASIC WRAP

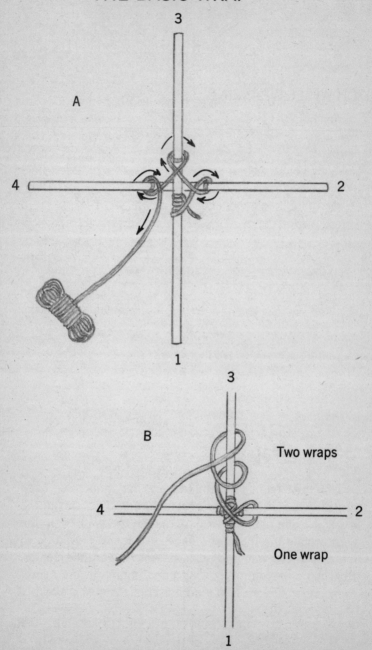

A

3

4

2

1

B

Two wraps

4

2

One wrap

3

1

yarn in your right hand, draw the strand of yarn *over* Arm 2, then pass it underneath and up around the stick. Arm 2 is now completely encircled. This is the basic wrap.

For this first time around the skeleton, it is best to wrap 2, so wrap Arm 2 again in the same way—over, under, and up—bringing the strand back into position to pass over Arm 3. Again, push the yarn toward the center with your index finger to reduce "give." Draw the yarn across Arm 3 and repeat the same procedure, wrapping the stick twice around. For Arm 4, if you twist your wrist toward you slightly you will be able to wrap the yarn without changing hands. Wrap Arm 4 twice, and you are ready to start a new round requiring only one wrap per arm. After you wrap a few rounds and secure the loose end of yarn, cut the end off. Note: If you are left-handed, reverse the entire procedure and wrap clockwise instead of counterclockwise as has been described.

Continue giving one wrap to each arm and the eye will appear. During the wrapping, if the weave starts to bunch

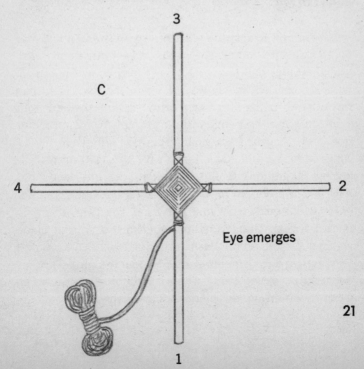

Eye emerges

up, wrap 2 for one or two rounds to allow more space to the weave.

When you finish weaving with one color, simply clove hitch and cut the yarn, leaving about ½″ to be concealed and held securely by the following stitches. *Always* start the new color on a different arm from the one you just wrapped. Continue the same wrapping procedure, beginning and ending the color with the clove hitch. Remember to wrap 3 or 4 on an arm, after making the beginning knot, to cover the loose end and to hold the knot steady. White glue may also be used on the back of the Ojo if necessary or desired. Try to wrap all arms approximately the same number of times to keep the colors of the design even. And *always* end a color on the same arm on which you started it. You may also wish to use the half hitch for the first two rounds after changing yarn to hold it taut.

Twirling

As you add wraps, the weaving expands and it may become awkward to hold the skeleton with one hand, wrap with the other and keep the proper tension in the weave. At this point, an easier way to string the yarn is to use the twirling method. Holding Arm 1 of the skeleton with your left hand, draw the yarn in front of Arm 2 with your right, as shown. Then hold the yarn with your thumb while grasping the stick just below the last wrap. Following illustrations **B** and **C,** switch your left hand from Arm 1 to the bottom of Arm 2, rotating the God's Eye figure. Hold Arm 2 with your left hand and twirl it around once between your fingertips, guiding the yarn in place with your right hand. Push the yarn toward the center. This makes one complete wrap. Repeat the procedure for each arm, twirling twice when it becomes necessary to wrap 2, or many times when winding for space.

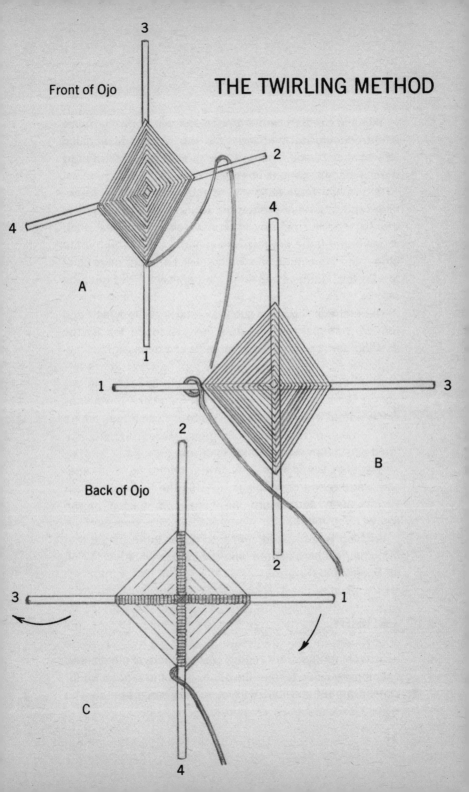

THE TWIRLING METHOD

Front of Ojo

A

B

Back of Ojo

C

Winding

Winding the yarn around each individual arm is a way of introducing open spaces into the weave. In addition to enhancing and "airing" the overall design, spacing makes many variations possible.

It is most important to wind the yarn tightly onto the arms and to measure often the width of the windings and the distance from the eye to the windings. If all the arms receive the same amount of winding, between the wrappings, the spacing in the weave will be equal all around the design. Unequal windings may cause the design to be askew.

Geometrical figures, such as stars, rectangles, diamonds, triangles and squares, may also be formed by winding certain arms for a distance and bypassing or giving other arms less winding. Here too, however, measurement is needed, or the square, triangle or rectangle will be crooked. Do not go strictly by number of windings since some windings may be slightly closer than others and some yarn may have thin spots. Measure and check the design often to see if it looks crooked.

Use glue when necessary at the beginning, but especially at the end of windings, to affix the following wraps into position and insure the continued tension of the weave.

Winding is also used simply to cover the arms so that the wood of the skeleton won't show, as when you finish off the ends of the arms.

Tension

Stretching the yarn tightly around the skeleton and keeping it pushed toward the center is necessary for keeping the proper tension. It is especially important as you

24

begin to weave and as you change yarns, in order to hold the springy material in place and prevent the weave from sagging. Use the half hitch and/or glue freely whenever the yarn shows signs of slipping. To test whether or not you are getting the right tension, pull the yarn as tightly as possible. This will be too tight, and may cause the sticks to bend or break. Now, loosen the yarn completely. Obviously, this is too loose. Naturally, the yarn should be stretched somewhere between these two extremes. The proper tension will be more tight than loose, and with a little practice you will achieve a good balance. Use your own judgment based on the way the yarn behaves.

With extremely large designs, proper tension is easier to achieve if you place the Ojo on a table and twirl the entire construction, alternating hands as you wrap. Note: Since each wrap on an arm rests against the previous one, it is extremely important to push the yarn toward the center of the Ojo after each wrap so that the yarn will not "give", later.

Use glue as often as you wish. It is essential to hold wrappings for proper weave tension, for spacings and for any geometric figure. Apply the glue to the back of the arms to keep it from showing through or staining the yarn in front. If you make a mistake, remove the glue with fingernail polish.

Measurement

When you change colors or go from one variation to another, measure the distance from the center of the eye to the end of the weaving on each arm. For the basic, diamond-shaped Ojo, be sure that the distances are equal on each arm. If they are not, you have not kept the tension the same on all wraps or you have not been pushing the yarn toward the center after each wrap. If the measurement is only slightly off, it may be adjusted by pushing the yarn on the long arm toward the center. Yarn may not be pushed too far, however, or the weave will loosen and sag. If the error is more than ¼" off, the wrappings must be undone, and you must start again from the point at which you went wrong.

Tassels and Pompoms

After the weaving is finished, the ends of the arms (if the weaving doesn't go that far) may be wrapped with yarn, painted or stained, or left as is. In any case, you may want to add tassels or pompoms.

To make tassels, wind yarn 15 to 35 times (depending on bulk of yarn and desired size) around a piece of cardboard. Next, slip a long strand, folded for strength, under one end of the yarn and tie and knot it. Cut the other end of the folded yarn, releasing the yarn from the cardboard. Make a topknot by winding another strand of yarn tightly around the top of the tassel. It should be placed from ¼" to one inch from the top of the tassel, depending on its thickness and length. Work the end of the winding strand into the windings with a pin, or thread it through a needle and sew it in. Trim the ends of the tassel to the desired length.

Pompoms are made much in the same way as tassels. First, wind the yarn around a piece of cardboard or your fingertips. Then remove the folded yarn and tie it very tightly in the middle with a long double strand, which will also be used to attach the pompom to the Ojo. Cut the folded yarn at both ends and fluff it into a ball.

Tassels and pompoms may be made using only one color of yarn, or strands of all of the colors used in the Ojo they are to decorate.

Loop for Hanging

Thread a long strand of yarn onto a needle or fold it in half for extra strength and work it through the weaving near the top of the Ojo. Knot the strands tightly in back, then knot again near the ends of the strands and you have an excellent loop for hanging the Ojo on a wall.

Weaving Variations

Back Wrap

The back wrap is very much a part of Ojo-making. It gives the design a three-dimensional effect since the back wrap weave rests on a lower level than the front wrap weave. It is worked by weaving the same basic wrap, but on the *reverse* side of the skeleton. To introduce the back wrap variation, simply turn the Ojo so that its back is toward you and wrap exactly as you have been doing on the front. Be sure to check the front at intervals to make sure that the arms are being completely covered. In addition to creating a beautiful figure, this variation helps to balance the tension on the front and the back. The back wrap variation may also be wrapped from the front. Simply wind the yarn *under*, then up, over and back around each arm as shown.

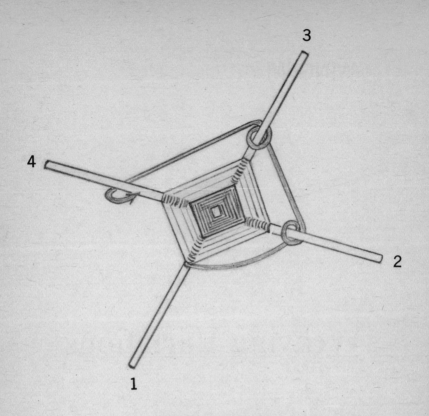

BACK WRAP

Wing Wrap

Wings open up space in the God's Eye design creating a very attractive effect. They are usually started immediately after the eye is established, but they can be made at any point. To get the maximum effect, use several colors.

Wings are formed by working the front wrap on opposing arms and bypassing consecutive arms. In other words,

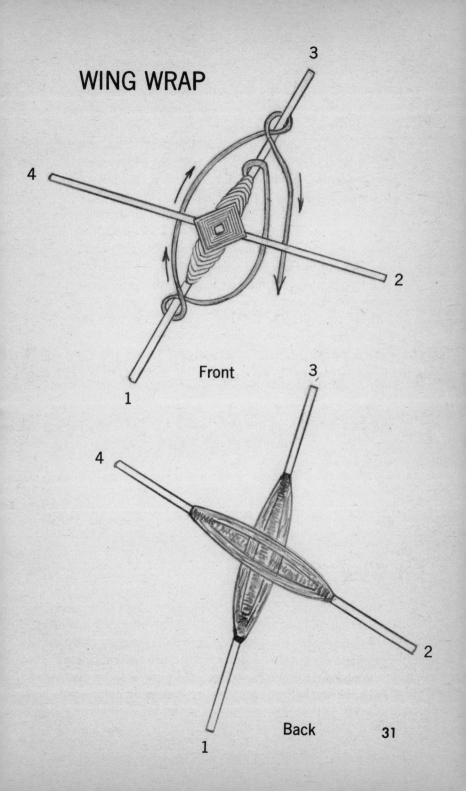

WING WRAP

3

4

2

1

Front

3

4

2

1

Back

31

on a basic, four-armed Ojo, you would wrap Arm 1, then Arm 3, then 1, then 3, and so on, as shown. When these wings reach the desired length, using as many colors as you like, knot and glue the yarn; then wrap Arms 2 and 4 in the same way. You will have a tighter and crisper design if you make each wrap a half hitch, but this is not mandatory. The yarn in front will form a V shape, while the yarn in back will stretch out parallel to the sticks being woven. Always complete one entire set of wings before starting the next. Measure the length of the wings from the center of the eye to the end of the wrappings to make sure that the wings are equal in length before proceeding to the next variation.

To create a cruciform design, one of the wings—usually the bottom one on Arm 1—must be longer than the other three arms. This is done by wrapping the long arm three or four times each round, while the other arms receive only a single or double wrap.

Wings can also be made to represent the petals of a flower by introducing a layered look. This variation looks

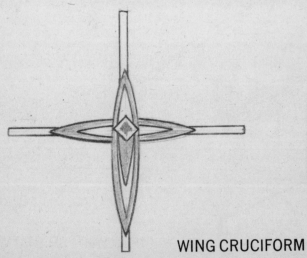

WING CRUCIFORM

best woven on a six- or eight-armed skeleton, for more petals. First, weave wings on a set of arms for a certain distance; then outline them with a different color. Repeat the procedure on the second, third, and fourth set of arms. When this first layer is completed, return to the first set of arms and wing wrap another two petals, and outline them. Repeat the procedure on the other sets of arms. When all the arms have two layers, you may start the third. You can make as many layers as you like.

Spider Web

If you are making rather long wings in a cross or a flower design, you may wish to fill in some of the empty space between the arms. A lovely spider web effect may be achieved by wrapping a single strand one round for each inch of wing completed, as shown. Go around at least three or four times at one-inch intervals to get the full effect.

FLOWER WITH SPIDER WEB

Double Weave

Suppose you want your God's Eye to look just as pre-sentable on the back as it does on the front. If you are planning to make a mobile, a desk model, a centerpiece, or a three-dimensional design, you will want to learn the double weave.

Hold the Ojo in front of you and wrap the arms one complete round. Returning to your starting point on Arm 1, twirl the entire skeleton to its rear side, wrap Arm 1, and go on to complete one round on this side. When you return to Arm 1 again, twirl the Ojo back to its original front side for the next round. Continue twirling the Ojo from front to back after each round to achieve a double weave.

Sandwich

Another form of double weaving gives the impression that the skeleton is sandwiched between two separate Ojos. For this variation, use an eight- or sixteen-armed skeleton and wrap every second arm (odd-numbered arms). Then turn the skeleton and wrap the uncovered (even-numbered) arms. This design is perfect for making Christmas tree ornaments with skeletons of pick-up sticks glued to cardboard centers.

Double Color—Double Weave

By wrapping two colors at the same time, as explained here, the Ojo will be half one color and half the other. First, make an eye about ½" wide (just enough to cover

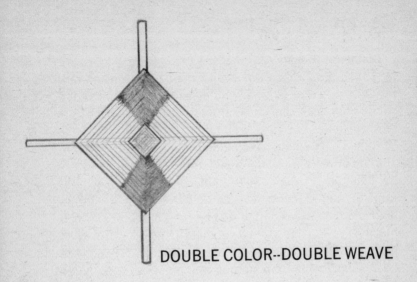

DOUBLE COLOR--DOUBLE WEAVE

the center). Then hitch two colors of yarn to the same arm. With one of the colors, wrap one round, alternating front and back wraps. In other words, wind the yarn *over* and around Arm 1, *under* and around Arm 2, *over* and around Arm 3, and *under* and around Arm 4. Return to Arm 1 and hold with a half hitch. Now, with the second color, reverse the wrapping; that is, wrap *under* and around Arm 1, *over* and around Arm 2, *under* and around Arm 3, and *over* and around Arm 4. Repeat until the design emerges. You may reverse the order of colors at this time for a new effect. Although this is a rather difficult weave, it is well worth the effort.

Geometric Shapes

Diamonds, hexagons, octagons, triangles and stars are all design possibilities when you extend your weaving with many extra wraps or when you construct skeletons in the shape of crosses and kites, or add additional sticks of different lengths.

To make an elongated diamond shape, wrap the bottom and top arms of a square cross (1 and 3) two or three extra times each round while continuing to wrap the side arms (2 and 4) once. You can control the shape of the diamond by increasing the number of extra wraps, which might go as high as six in a very elongated figure. The half hitch and glue are needed when the stitches expand. The best results come from starting with one extra wrap (wrap 2) for a few times, then wrap 3, 4, 5, etc., so that the pattern emerges gradually and the strands of yarn separate only slightly with each stitch. The kite is made in the same way, except that only Arm 1 is given extra wraps; Arms 2, 3 and 4 receive the usual one. The kite figure, however, can also be shaped so that the sides extend somewhat but not quite as much as the bottom.

A hexagon emerges when you notch and assemble three equally spaced sticks into a skeleton. The octagon is achieved by making a skeleton of four equally spaced sticks. A four-point star makes use of the octagon skeleton except that the extra sticks are smaller and shorter. The Star of David requires the same smaller and shorter sticks, but they must be placed at a 22° angle.

Many other shapes may be designed and used for Ojo-making. Detailed instructions for making various geometric shapes are included in the Ojo Projects section of this book.

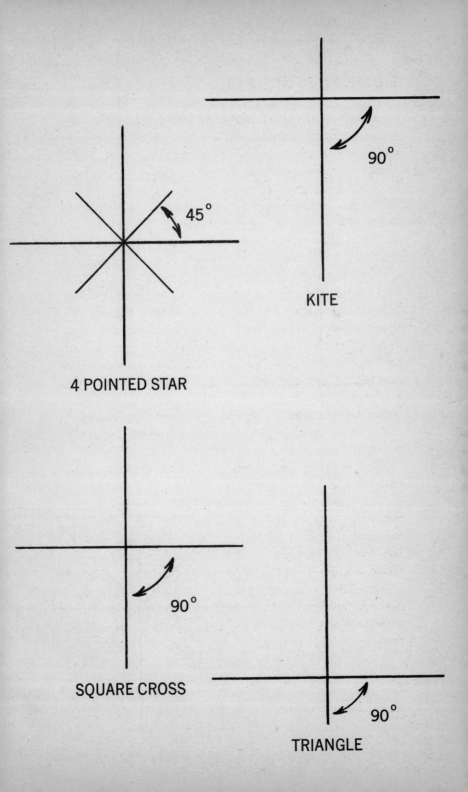

90°

KITE

45°

4 POINTED STAR

90°

SQUARE CROSS

90°

TRIANGLE

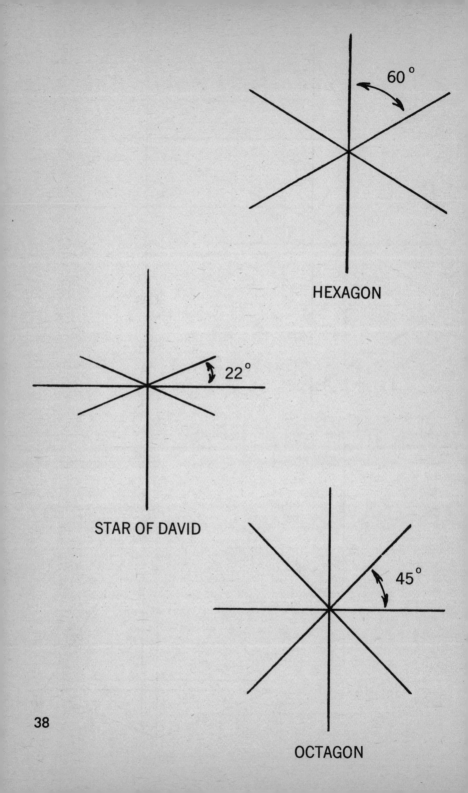

HEXAGON

60°

STAR OF DAVID

22°

OCTAGON

45°

38

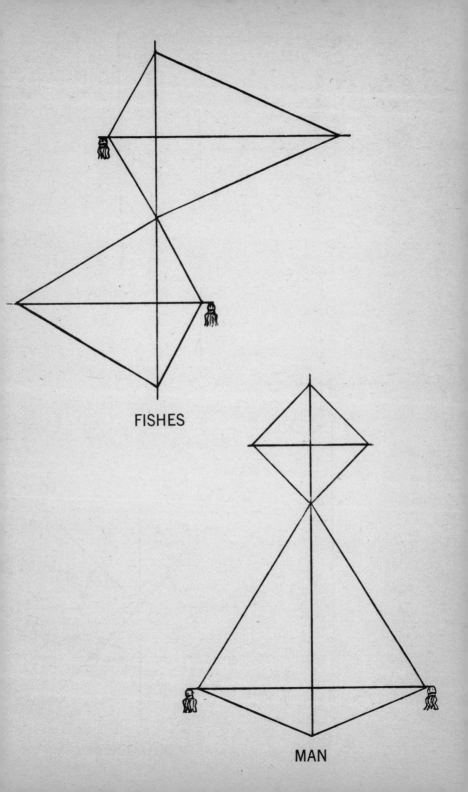

FISHES

MAN

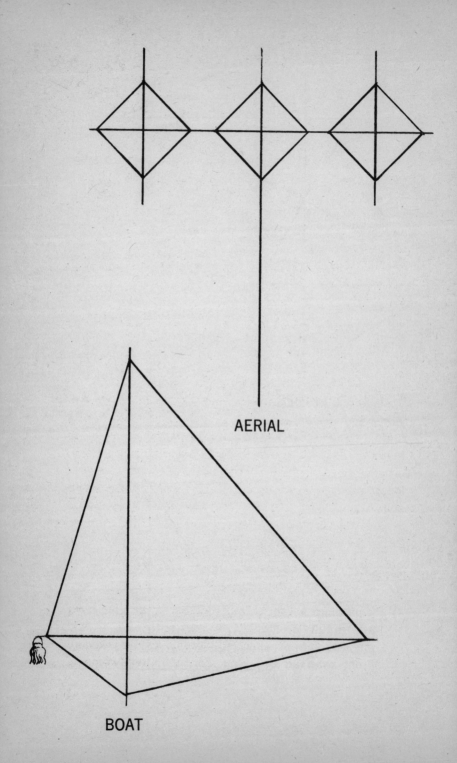

AERIAL

BOAT

Mini-Ojos

Since you have now learned how to do the basic Ojo wraps and variations, you are probably anxious to work a project. You may prefer, however, to start off small, using materials available right now in your sewing basket, kitchen and closet. So here are a number of mini-Ojo project ideas, perfect for testing out your newfound Ojo-crafting abilities and, later, your own original designs.

Practice Ideas

1) Glue three flat toothpicks together so that the arms are equally spaced. Use crochet thread, crewel mending yarn or other fine material for the weaving. Front wrap an eye, then continue front wrapping

changing colors once or twice. Make a loop at the top for hanging, using needle and thread if more convenient.

2) Glue ice cream sticks or sugar stirrers together into an octagon or hexagon. Using thin yarn, try the petal pattern with spider web. Adjust the spacing between the web strands to the length of the arms. Make and attach small fluffy pompoms. Attach loop and hang.

3) Find eight or sixteen small sticks, such as toothpicks, sugar stirrers, pick-up sticks, or bamboo hors d'oeuvre skewers, and glue them securely to a small piece of cardboard so that they extend outward like spokes in a wheel. This forms your skeleton. Do the double weave or sandwich variation with mohair or sport yarn. Add beads, sequins, stars or glitter to decorate.

4) Using a tinker toy or cork or styrofoam ball as an eye, insert sticks up to 12″ in length. Decorate the center with a small mirror, a birthstone or jewel, a piece of felt or printed material, a magazine illustration, or Indian beads mounted on leather. Try the double color —double weave, using colors that go well with the eye of the Ojo. Make and attach two-colored tassels.

5) Make a number of ice cream stick Ojos using the same three or four colors but different variations and designs and suspend them three or four inches apart from a long twisted strand made up of the colors.

6) Make a Christmas angel. Notch and glue two ¼″ dowels, three or four inches in length, into a kite design. Keep the weaving on Arm 3 at a minimum, giving Arms 2 and 4 some extra wraps and Arm 1 the most wrapping. Use soft white yarn and thin strands

of gold cord in the design. Attach a bead or small styrofoam ball to Arm 3 for the head. Features may be painted onto the bead, or small bead or sequin features may be attached to the styrofoam ball with small pins. Glue on a gold cord halo. Attach loop and hang.

7) Make a snowman centerpiece. Onto a nine-inch-long ⅜″ dowel, notch and glue a three-inch-long dowel one and one-half inches from the top, and a five-inch-long dowel three and one-half inches from the bottom, a variation of the MAN shape on page 39. Double weave the two separate Ojos on the long dowel. Use rather heavy white yarn, weave tightly and wrap to the ends of all except Arm 1. Glue craft paper features (and pipe?) onto smaller top head Ojo, and black craft paper buttons onto lower body Ojo. Affix Arm 1 of Ojos onto stand and cover stand with cotton snow.

8) Make a number of flower Ojos, using the wing layered variation and outlining petals, for a bouquet. Make different size and shape Ojos for variety and use colors that go together in one flower: light and dark shades of pink, blue and purple, and brown center yellow petals, black center white petals, etc. Flowers may be mounted on wire stems wrapped in green yarn.

Uses

As you have already seen, there are a great many ways to use the Ojo de Dios, some extremely practical, all enormously decorative. A mini-Ojo, however, as a personal good luck charm, is at home anywhere. It may be attached to a key chain or watch fob, or a choker necklace, or worn on a headband, armband or garter as an amulet. A number of Ojos may also be attached to a wide, fashionable, suede or leather belt.

In the home, mini-Ojos may be strung and hung as a garland over an entranceway, as party or holiday decorations, even affixed to a background and framed. (The Ojo flower bouquet, for instance, makes a lovely framed picture.) An Ojo may be attached to a pencil or pen, used to call attention to bulletin board messages, or sewn to a ribbon for an interesting bookmark.

A specially handcrafted blue and white or pink and white Ojo mobile makes a lovely decorative charm for a new baby's nursery. It must always be hung out of baby's reach, however.

A once-worked Ojo design that has become a favorite, may be quickly transferred to canvas and worked in needlepoint, changing shades slightly to keep the three-dimensional look of front and back wraps.

Every day, as the knowledge of Ojo-making spreads across the country, new uses and applications are being discovered. Perhaps you will be the first to use an Eye of God in an original and creative way. All you have to do is look around you and start.

Ojo Projects

If you are not yet ready to set off on your own to create original designs, or if you simply prefer a little guidance, here are a selection of nineteen Ojo projects, which can be easily adapted to fit individual tastes. Although specific numbers of wraps are given in the directions (which have all been tested), keep in mind that each Ojo craftsman has a different touch—a tighter or looser weave. If the directions seem to indicate too much or too little wrapping for your own touch, but the tension is correct, adjust the number of wraps or rounds accordingly.

Colors of your choice may also be substituted for those suggested, and the length and width of the sticks may be changed so that the project will make use of the skeleton materials available, or may fit any space, and serve any specific need.

45

The Spur

Materials

Two 36″ dowels ⅜″ in diameter, cut into 27″ and 26″ lengths
One 36″ dowel 5/16″ in diameter, cut into four 7″ lengths
Suggested yarn colors: red, white and black (1 oz. each)

Step 1: Measure and notch long dowels in the middle. Place the 26″ dowel horizontal, the 27″ dowel vertical, and glue them together at the notch. Make notches 3¼″ from the end of each arm for the small Ojos, but don't glue on the short lengths until the central Ojo is finished.

Step 2: For eye, front wrap with red until eye measures 2˝.

Step 3: Front wrap 10 rounds black

8 rounds red	12 rounds red
4 rounds black	10 rounds black
3 rounds white	3 rounds white
4 rounds black	10 rounds black

10 rounds red

Step 4: Continue wrapping last band of red until Ojo measures 13˝ x 13˝. If slightly uneven, place extra wrappings on short arms and/or push wrappings on slightly long arms toward center to attain desired symmetrical shape.

Step 5: Wind Arms 2 and 4 with red for 1¼˝.

Step 6: Wind Arm 1 with black for 1¼˝.

Step 7: Wind Arm 3 with black for 2˝.

Step 8: Glue 7˝ dowels in place at notches and let dry.

Step 9: For small Ojos, on Arms 2 and 4, front wrap eye with red for 1˝, then wrap 2 rounds white, 10 rounds black, 2 rounds white and finish with red, until weaving measures about 3½˝ square.

Step 10: Wind remaining exposed wood on these two arms with red.

Step 11: Add loop for hanging on Arm 3.

Step 12: Make small Ojos on Arms 1 and 3, wrapping eye with black for 1˝. Then wrap 10 rounds red, 3 rounds white, and finish with black until weaving measures about 3½˝ square.

Step 13: Wind remaining exposed wood on these two arms with black.

Note: Spur Ojo used to illustrate this project was woven on a skeleton of cottonwood tree branches.

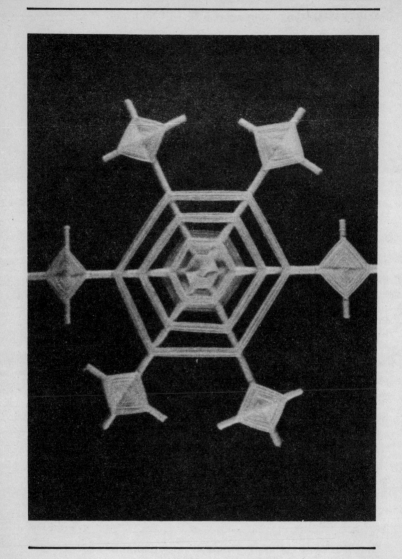

Snowflake

Materials

Three 36" dowels 5/16" in diameter
Suggested yarn color: white or pastel (1 oz.) Use 4-ply yarn or mohair

Step 1: Cut three dowels 18" in length, notch them in the middle and glue them together so that they are equally spaced. Make a notch two inches from the end of each arm.

Step 2: Cut six dowels 4½" in length, notch them in the middle and set them aside.

Step 3: For eye, front wrap all arms until eye measures 1¾". Push the yarn tightly toward the center so that no wood shows.

Step 4: Back wrap 12 rounds.
Front wrap 6 rounds.
Back wrap 8 rounds.

Step 5: Wind all arms ½" for spacing.
Step 6: Front wrap 7 rounds.
Step 7: Wind all arms ½".
Step 8: Front wrap 7 rounds.
Step 9: Wind all arms about 1¼", or until yarn reaches 4½" from end of arms.

Step 10: Glue on 4½" dowels at notches. When dry, make small Ojos, 2½" square, on each skeleton. Wind all arms (covering exposed wood) and use glue to hold the yarn in place.

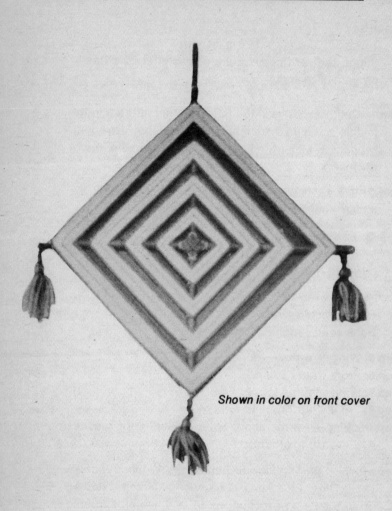

Shown in color on front cover

Raincloud

Materials

One 36″ dowel 5/16″ in diameter, cut in half, notched and glued to form a square cross

Suggested yarn colors: off-white, black and turquoise (1 oz. each)

Step 1: For eye, front wrap with turquoise until eye measures 1½″. Add 2 rounds white.

Step 2: Back wrap 5 rounds black

Step 3: Front wrap 4 rounds white
3 rounds turquoise
4 rounds white

Step 4: Back wrap 6 rounds black

Step 5: Front wrap 5 rounds white
3 rounds turquoise
5 rounds white

Step 6: Back wrap 8 rounds black

Step 7: Front wrap 6 rounds white
3 rounds turquoise
6 rounds white

Step 8: Back wrap 10 rounds black

Step 9: Add loop for hanging on Arm 3.

Step 10: Front wrap 7 rounds white
3 rounds turquoise
7 rounds white

Step 11: Wind arms with turquoise to ends, glue and add tassels.

Sunbeam

Materials

Two 36´´ dowels ⅜´´ in diameter cut to lengths of 24´´, notched and glued to form a square cross
Suggested yarn colors: yellow, dark gold, melon and scarlet (1 oz. each)

Step 1: For eye, front wrap 3 rounds yellow
1 round melon
1 round scarlet
5 rounds yellow
1 round melon
1 round scarlet
1 round melon

Step 2: Back wrap 4 rounds yellow
4 rounds dark gold
4 rounds yellow

Step 3: Front wrap 2 rounds scarlet
2 rounds melon
2 rounds scarlet

Step 4: Wind all arms 6 times with dark gold to insert space, glue.

Step 5: Front wrap 2 rounds yellow
3 rounds melon

Step 6: Back wrap 5 rounds dark gold
2 rounds yellow
5 rounds dark gold

Step 7: Front wrap 3 rounds scarlet
2 rounds yellow

Step 8: Wind all arms 12 times with yellow, glue.

Step 9: Front wrap 4 rounds melon
3 rounds scarlet
4 rounds melon

Step 10: Back wrap 18 rounds yellow
Step 11: Wind all arms 18 times with yellow, glue.

Step 12: Back wrap 5 rounds yellow
5 rounds melon
3 rounds scarlet

Step 13: Continue back wrapping with dark gold until arms are completely covered. Use glue freely for the last 2˝.

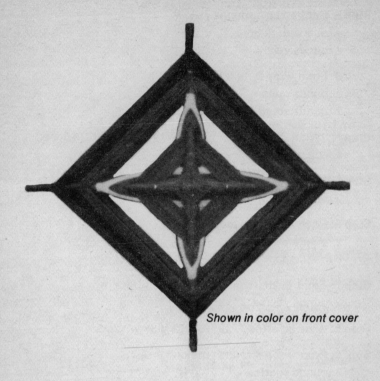

Shown in color on front cover

Blue Lake

Materials

One 36″ dowel 5/16″ in diameter, cut in half, notched and glued to form a square cross

Suggested yarn colors: cobalt blue, cardinal red, kelly green and white (1 oz. blue, ½ oz. each others)

Step 1: For eye, front wrap 5 rounds blue
  2 rounds green
  2 rounds red

Step 2: Wing wrap 2 rounds green
  2 rounds red
  3 rounds blue

Step 3: Back wrap 5 rounds blue
  2 rounds green
  2 rounds red
  6 rounds blue

Step 4: Wing wrap 5 rounds green
  2 rounds red
  6 rounds blue
  8 rounds white

Step 5: Back wrap 5 rounds blue

Step 6: Front wrap 2 rounds green
  2 rounds red
  2 rounds green

Step 7: Back wrap 10 rounds blue
Step 8: Add loop for hanging on Arm 3.

Step 9: Front wrap 2 rounds green
  2 rounds red
  2 rounds green

Step 10: Back wrap 10 rounds blue
Step 11: Front wrap 8 rounds green
Step 12: Wind all arms to ends with blue.

Mesa

Materials

Two 26″ dowels ⅜″ in diameter, cut to lengths of
24″ and 28″

Suggested yarn colors: burnt orange, purple, olive
green and dark gold (1 oz. each)

Step 1: Place 24″ dowel horizontal to 28″, notch and glue
to form a square cross. Let dry.

Step 2: For eye, front wrap burnt orange until eye measures 1″. Then front wrap 1 round dark gold and 3 rounds purple.

Step 3: Back wrap 10 rounds burnt orange.

Step 4: Wind all arms with purple 8 times (purple should show when you begin wing wrap).

Step 5: Wing wrap 6 rounds dark gold.

Step 6: Back wrap 12 rounds purple.

Step 7: Front wrap 3 rounds burnt orange.

Step 8: Wind all arms with purple 6 times.

Step 9: Wind all arms with dark gold 10 times.

Step 10: Wing wrap 24 rounds olive green on Arms 1 and 3; 12 rounds dark gold on Arms 2 and 4. Measure. Wrappings on Arms 1 and 3 should extend 7″ from center of eye. Wrappings on Arms 2 and 4 should extend 6″.

Step 11: Front wrap 10 rounds dark gold
3 rounds olive green

Step 12: Back wrap 5 rounds burnt orange
2 rounds purple
3 rounds burnt orange
2 rounds purple
8 rounds burnt orange

Step 13: Front wrap 3 rounds olive green
10 rounds dark gold
3 rounds olive green
10 rounds dark gold
3 rounds olive green

Step 14: Add loop for hanging on Arm 3.

Step 15: Wind all arms with orange, glue at ends and add orange and purple tassels 7″ long.

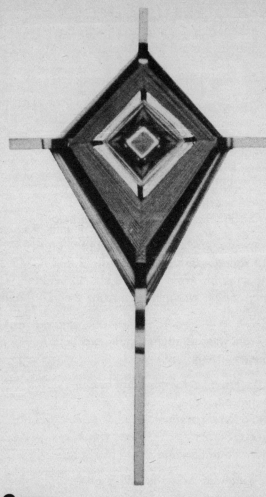

La Cruz

Materials

Any flat sticks ¾″ wide, ½″ deep, cut to lengths of 22″ and 30″

Suggested yarn colors: black, white, kelly green and multi-green (1 oz. kelly green, ½ oz. other)

Step 1: Notch 30″ stick 11″ from end. Notch 22″ stick in the middle; glue to form cruciform. If desired, shape the ends of the arms to an angle or point and paint or stain.

Step 2: For eye, front wrap with green until eye measures 2″. Then wrap 3 rounds white.

Step 3: Front wrap 3 rounds black (wrap 2 or 3 each arm to separate strands about ¼″).

Step 4: Wing wrap 6 rounds green, or until wing measures ½″.

Step 5: Front wrap 6 rounds multi-green.

Step 6: Wing wrap 12 rounds black, or until wing measures 1″.

Step 7: To form extended kite shape, front wrap green as follows: Arms 2, 3 and 4 should receive single wraps, while Arm 1 receives single wraps for 2″, then wrap 2 several times; then extend wrapping on Arm 1 to wrap 3. Continue wrapping rounds until Arm 1 measures 4½″ from beginning to end of green wrappings. Green wrappings on Arms 2, 3 and 4 should measure approximately 2″.

Step 8: Back wrap 10 rounds black, or until Arms 2, 3 and 4 measure 1″. Continue wrap 3 on Arm 1.

Step 9: Add loop on Arm 3 for hanging.

Step 10: Change to multi-green and wrap 10 rounds or more, continuing single wrappings on Arm 3 and wrap 3 on Arm 1. Half hitch often throughout and use glue to hold the yarn in kite shape.

Step 11: Glue and cut yarn, then work or sew loose ends into wrappings with pin or needle. Leave wood (painted, stained or natural) exposed.

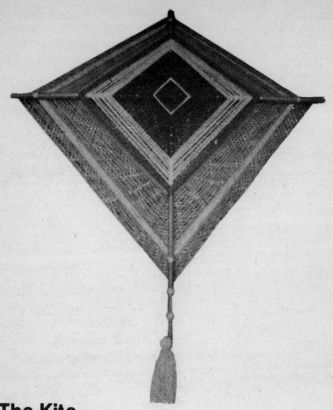

The Kite

Materials

Two 36″ dowels 5/16″ in diameter, cut to lengths of 22″

Suggested yarn colors: maroon, yellow, purple and medium blue (½ oz. each)

Step 1: Notch one dowel 5½″ from end; notch second dowel in center. Glue together to form a kite-shaped skeleton.

Step 2: For eye, front wrap maroon for 2″, then wrap 3. rounds yellow.

Step 3: Front wrap maroon, wrapping Arm 3 once each round, but wrap 2 Arms 1, 2 and 4 for about 1″. Kite shape will start to emerge. Continue front wrapping maroon, extending Arm 3 wrappings to wrap 2, and Arms 1, 2 and 4 to wrap 3.

Step 4: Keep adjusting the wraps until the maroon measures (from the center of the eye to the end of the weaving) Arm 3—2½″, Arms 2 and 4—3½″ and Arm 1—4″.

Step 5: Change to yellow and front wrap 8 rounds. Continue to wrap 2 on Arm 3 and wrap 3 on other arms.

Step 6: Change to purple. Front wrap four rounds, giving Arm 3 single wraps, Arms 2 and 4 wrap 3, and Arm 1 wrap 4, until weaving measures 13″ long and 11″ wide. Adjust wraps accordingly.

Step 7: Add loop for hanging on Arm 3.

Step 8: Change to blue and begin back wrap. Use glue as you back wrap 4 on Arms 2 and 4, back wrap 5 on Arm 2 and single wrap Arm 3, until 1″ from ends of Arms 2 and 4. Leave 2½″ to 3″ of Arm 1 bare.

Step 9: Give Ojo a trimming of yellow by single wrapping 4 rounds. Use half hitch and glue to keep shape.

Step 10: Finish front wrapping blue, giving extra wrappings as in Step 8, until the end of Arm 3 is reached. Wrap the exposed wood on Arm 1 with blue yarn. Make and hang a tassel from it. The topknot should be made to touch the end of the arm. Or, if you prefer, paint the end and add a huge pompom instead.

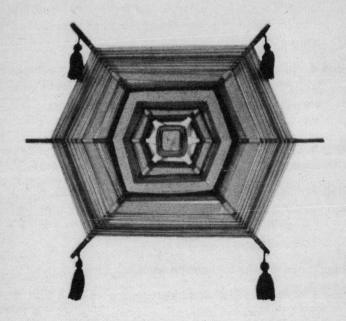

Satellite

Materials

Three 36˝ dowels ⅜˝ or ½˝ in diameter
Suggested yarn colors: wood brown, bright gold, red
and copper (½ oz. red, 1½ oz. other)

Step 1: Notch and glue dowels together at 60° angles; two
dowels crossing in front of third vertical dowel.

Step 2: For eye, front wrap gold for 1″ on four top, crossed arms (2, 3, 5 and 6). Continue to front wrap four arms only, adding 4 rounds brown
   2 rounds red
   2 rounds gold
   10 rounds brown

Step 3: Wing wrap 12 rounds gold

Step 4: Back wrap 3 rounds copper. (For rest of design, all arms receive wraps.)
   5 rounds red
   10 rounds gold

Step 5: Front wrap 3 rounds copper
   8 rounds red
   12 rounds gold

Step 6: Back wrap 10 rounds copper
   8 rounds red
   14 rounds gold

Step 7: Front wrap 10 rounds brown
   4 rounds gold
   3 rounds red
   4 rounds gold
   10 rounds brown

Step 8: Back wrap 20 rounds copper

Step 9: Front wrap 15 rounds brown
   5 rounds gold
   2 rounds red
   5 rounds gold
   15 rounds brown

Step 10: Back wrap copper until design reaches desired size.

Step 11: Wind all arms with any color yarn desired; glue. Add tassels or pompoms.

Shown in color on back cover

Warrior Shield

Materials

Four 36″ dowels 5/16″ or ⅜″ in diameter, cut in half
Suggested yarn colors: cobalt blue, medium blue, red and off-white (1 oz. each)
A 2″ or 3″ circular Indian bead design—sew beads on a cloth or leather background or buy a ready-made rosette from a handicraft shop. (You may want to carry out the colors of the rosette in your design.)
Fluffy feathers or cotton balls (optional)

Step 1: Notch and glue dowels together at 45° angles to form octagon. Number the arms counterclockwise starting with the one at the bottom.

Step 2: Since the eye is to be covered with the rosette bead design, merely wind the arms with white yarn so that the wood won't show. Attach the beadwork to the center of the skeleton with glue and/or thread. Next, front wrap white yarn around the rosette on all the arms until a frame emerges—about 5 rounds.

Step 3: Wing wrap for 1″ with white, then trim with 2 rounds of cobalt blue.

Step 4: Front wrap 3 rounds red
8 rounds white
4 rounds medium blue
8 rounds white
3 rounds red

Step 5: Wing wrap for 1″ with white, trim with 2 rounds of cobalt blue.

Step 6: Front wrap 3 rounds medium blue
8 rounds white
4 rounds cobalt blue
8 rounds white
3 rounds medium blue

Step 7: Wing wrap for 1″ with white, trim with 2 rounds of cobalt blue.

Step 8: Front wrap 3 rounds cobalt blue
8 rounds white
4 rounds red
8 rounds white
3 rounds cobalt blue

Step 9: Wind ends of arms, if not covered with wrappings, with white; glue.

Step 10: Glue fluffy feathers or balls of cotton to ends of arms, if desired.

Shown in color on back cover

Squash Blossom

Materials

Four 36″ dowels ⅜″ in diameter, cut to lengths of 26″

Suggested yarn colors: burnt orange, olive green, taupe or tan and dark brown (1 oz. each)

Step 1: Notch and glue dowels together at 45° angles to form octagon. Number arms counterclockwise starting with arm at the bottom.

Step 2: For eye, front wrap burnt orange for 1½˝ on Arms 1, 3, 5 and 7 only. Then front wrap these four arms with 2 rounds taupe
2 rounds dark brown
3 rounds orange

Step 3: Next, on Arms 2, 4, 6 and 8, front wrap
6 rounds orange
4 rounds taupe
3 rounds dark brown

Step 4: Wing wrap 3˝ with orange to form a flower figure. Finish one set of wings before beginning the next.

Step 5: Back wrap 20 rounds of olive green on Arms 1, 3, 5 and 7.

Step 6: Front wrap 3 rounds of olive green on Arms 2, 4, 6 and 8.

Step 7: Front wrap all arms with 3 rounds dark brown
15 rounds taupe
3 rounds dark brown

Step 8: Back wrap 12 rounds dark brown. Continue wrapping all arms throughout rest of design.

Step 9: Front wrap 3 rounds dark brown
15 rounds orange

Step 10: Back wrap 12 rounds dark brown
Step 11: Front wrap 15 rounds olive green
Step 12: Back wrap 12 rounds dark brown
Step 13: Front wrap 15 rounds orange
Step 14: Add loop for hanging.

Step 15: Back wrap dark brown until ends of arms are reached. Use glue for last 2˝.

Step 16: Add multi-colored pompoms.
Note: Use 36˝ dowels, thus extending the design, if you wish.

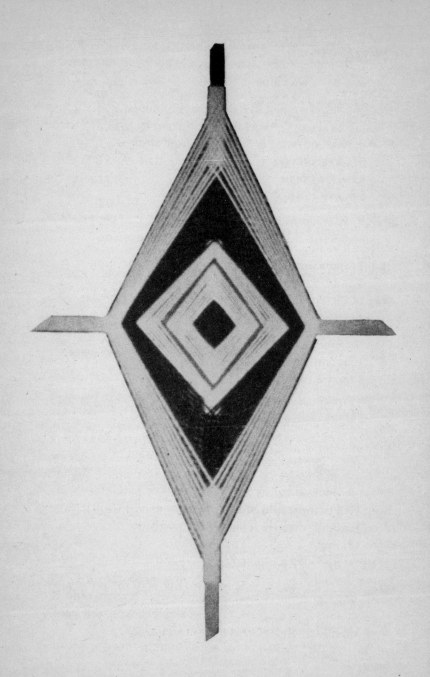

68

Hurucan

Materials

Any sticks about ¾″ wide by ½″ deep, cut to lengths of 30″ and 17″, notched and glued to form a square cross

Suggested yarn colors: off-white, dark gold and burgundy or wine rose (½ oz. each)

Black paint

Step 1: Paint the ends of the sticks black.

Step 2: For eye, front wrap burgundy for 1½″.

Step 3: Front wrap 10 rounds white. Wrap 2 Arms 1 and 3, and single wrap Arms 2 and 4. Strands on top and bottom should separate slightly and diamond shape will emerge.

Step 4: Front wrap 2 rounds dark gold close to white leaving no space between.

Step 5: Wrap 6 rounds white. Single wrap Arms 2 and 4, but wrap 3 on Arms 1 and 3.

Step 6: Wrap 8 rounds burgundy. Arms 2 and 4 continue to receive single wrap, but increase wrappings on Arms 1 and 3 from wrap 3 to wrap 6 as the diamond extends. Be sure the strands of the weave separate and stand alone. Glue must be used freely to hold the design and half hitch if necessary.

Step 7: Add loop for hanging to Arm 3.

Step 8: Continue front wrapping with white for 10 to 12 rounds. Arms 1 and 3 continue to receive wrap 6, while Arms 2 and 4 receive single wraps. Cut yarn, glue and conceal yarn ends in wrappings.

Christmas Tree

Materials

Two 36″ dowels ⅜″ in diameter, cut to lengths of 24″ and 18″

Suggested yarn colors: dark brown (long strand) and green (1½ oz.) and gold cord (optional)

Wooden (painted or stained as preferred) or styrofoam base

Gold and silver beads or sequins (optional)

Step 1: Notch the 24″ dowel 6″ from one end and notch the 18″ dowel in the middle. Glue at notches and let dry. Set short arm of triangular skeleton into base and glue.

Step 2: Hitch green yarn to Arm 2 (Arm 1 forms trunk of tree) and begin double weave. Wrap 2 Arms 2 and 4, and wrap 3 Arm 3 to get the long, triangular, tree shape. Glue all wraps in place.

Step 3: At the end of the first round, when you finish wrapping Arm 4, twirl the skeleton to its reverse side and front wrap Arms 4, 3 and 2 as directed. Twirl the skeleton again, as you finish wrapping Arm 2, and you will be working the double weave.

Step 4: Continue wrapping green, adding extra wraps to Arm 3 as the work progresses to separate the weave, to the ends of the arms. You may add a border of gold cord at this point. Stripes of gold cord may also be introduced into the green wrappings at 6″ intervals (as measured on Arm 3) if desired.

Step 5: Wind Arm 1 (the trunk of the tree) with brown, or paint or stain.

Step 6: Decorate tree with beads, sequins or other such materials if desired.

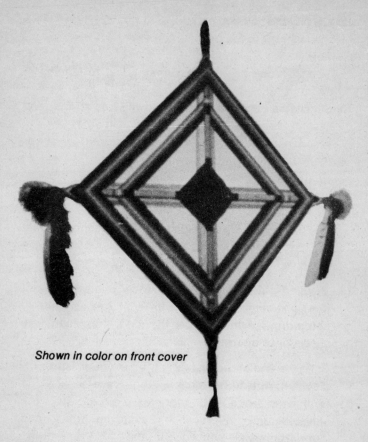

Shown in color on front cover

Zia

Materials

Two flat sticks ½″ or ¾″ square, 40″ in length
Round mirror from 4″ to 5″ in diameter
Four long feathers, red or white with black tips
Fluffy feathers
Small piece of leather, black leather lacing (optional)
Suggested yarn colors: black, scarlet, tangerine and
medium orange (1 oz. each)

Step 1: Notch sticks in the middle to form a square cross. Glue mirror to the center of crossed, glued sticks.

Step 2: Back wrap black yarn until weave extends 1½" from edge of mirror and gives it a frame.

Step 3: Wind all arms with tangerine for 5".

Step 4: Back wrap 10 rounds black
3 rounds scarlet
2 rounds tangerine
2 rounds medium orange
2 rounds tangerine
3 rounds scarlet

Step 5: Wind all arms with tangerine for 1¼".

Step 6: Front wrap 7 rounds black
3 rounds scarlet
3 rounds tangerine
2 rounds medium orange
3 rounds tangerine
3 rounds scarlet

Step 7: Back wrap 16 rounds black
Step 8: Wing wrap 5 rounds medium orange
4 rounds tangerine
2 rounds scarlet
Draw yarn tightly from arm to arm. Make each strand parallel to the next to form a flat, ribbon effect.

Step 9: Finish off Arms 2 and 4 by winding black yarn to ends and gluing. Affix long feathers in place by gluing, and wind securely with several wraps of yarn. Glue fluffy feathers over yarn and ends of feathers to conceal unsightliness.

Step 10: Finish off Arms 1 and 3 by gluing leather (cut to fit) to wood and tying lacing to give shoelace effect.

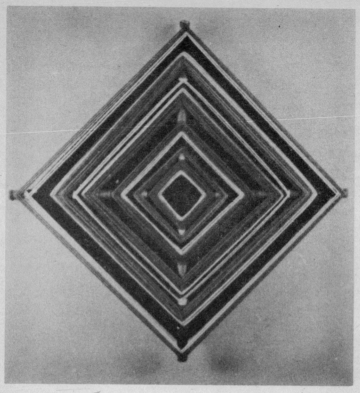

Pueblo

Materials

One 36″ dowel 5/16″ in diameter, cut into two 14″ lengths, notched and glued to form a square cross
Suggested yarn colors: black, white, red, turquoise and gold (½ oz. each)

Step 1: For eye, front wrap black until eye measures 1½″.

Step 2: Front wrap 4 rounds white
    4 rounds red

Step 3: Back wrap 4 rounds white
    4 rounds turquoise

Step 4: Front wrap 2 rounds turquoise
    2 rounds gold
    2 rounds black
    3 rounds white
    3 rounds red
    2 rounds turquoise

Step 5: Back wrap 12 rounds gold

Step 6: Front wrap 3 rounds turquoise
    2 rounds red
    2 rounds turquoise
    2 rounds white
    2 rounds black
    2 rounds white

Step 7: Back wrap 10 rounds red

Step 8: Front wrap 2 rounds turquoise
    3 rounds gold
    2 rounds red
    3 rounds white
    2 rounds black

Step 9: Back wrap 10 rounds black or wrap black until yarn reaches ½″ from the end of the arms. Place glue on back of wood before going on to next step.

Step 10: Front wrap 2 rounds white
    3 rounds red

Step 11: Add a loop for hanging on Arm 3.

Shown in color on back cover

Star of David

Materials

One 36″ dowel ⅜″ in diameter, cut in half
One 36″ dowel 5/16″ in diameter, cut into two 9″ lengths (half the dowel will be left over)
Suggest yarn colors: white, medium blue, dark blue and multi-blue (1 oz. each.)

Step 1: Notch and glue 18″ dowels in the middle to form a square cross. Notch and glue 9″ dowels in the middle and notch and glue them to the back of the longer dowels at 22° angles to the side arms. (See skeleton shape illustration on page 38.)

Step 2: For eye, front wrap white until eye measures 1″. Then front wrap 4 rounds of medium blue.

Step 3: Wind long side arms (3 and 7) for 1″ with white yarn.

Step 4: Back wrap only short arms (2, 4, 6 and 8) with white until a rectangle measuring 1½″ x 3½″ is formed. Then back wrap 5 rounds of medium blue.

Step 5: Wind long Arms 1 and 5 (top and bottom) with dark blue for 4″

Step 6: Front wrap only short arms (2, 4, 6 and 8) with dark blue until rectangle reaches ¼″ from ends of short arms.

Step 7: Make the Star of David by front wrapping 3 rounds of white yarn from Arm 1 (long) to Arms 4 and 6 (short, upper) to form a triangle. Repeat, making another triangle on Arms 8 and 2 (short, lower) and

Arm 5 (long). Glue wraps in place. The white star should extend to the tips of the short arms and leave no wood showing.

Step 8: Back wrap only long arms (1, 3, 5 and 7) with dark blue to make a diamond shape behind the star. The first wrap should rest alongside the edge of the top and bottom points of the star. Adjust wraps on Arms 3 and 7 accordingly. Wrap until blue yarn reaches the ends of the four points of the star woven on the short arms. Add extra wraps when necessary to achieve the proper shape.

Step 9: Check the photo above to make sure the design is correct so far. Next, front wrap 6 rounds of dark blue. This will frame the star and cover any unsightliness of the star design.

Step 10: Continue front wrapping 6 rounds using multi-blue yarn and giving extra wraps to separate the strands. Next, front wrap 3 rounds of dark blue.

Step 11: Back wrap 7 rounds multi-blue

Step 12: Front wrap 2 rounds white
3 rounds dark blue
10 rounds multi-blue (or until yarn reaches end of arms.)

Step 13: Add loop for hanging to Arm 5.

Evening Star

Materials

Two 36″ dowels ⅜″ in diameter.
One 36″ dowel 5/16″ in diameter, cut in half
Suggested yarn colors: dark brown, bright gold and
taupe (1 oz. each of 4-ply, single-strand), dark gold
and rust (2 oz. each of 5-ply, multi-strand), and a
multi-strand, multicolor consisting of one ply each of
black, rust and tangerine and two plies of bright yellow (2 oz.). May be ordered from a yarn specialty
shop.

Step 1: Notch all dowels in the middle and glue together at 45° angles. The short (18″) dowels should form an **X** in back of the crossed 36″ dowels to make an octagon skeleton. Middle dowels should be notched on both front and back.

Step 2: For eye, front wrap dark brown for 1″ on the four long arms (1, 3, 5 and 7) in front. Add multicolor until eye is 2½″ wide.

Step 3: Back wrap all 8 arms with dark gold until a background emerges and extends about 1½″ from the edge of the eye. Back wrap short arms (2, 4, 6 and 8) with rust for 2″.

Step 4: Wing wrap 6 rounds dark brown on long arms (1 and 5, 3 and 7)
3 rounds bright gold
3 rounds rust
4 rounds dark gold

Step 5: Back wrap 5 rounds multicolor on all arms.
Step 6: Front wrap 3 rounds dark brown on all arms.

Step 7: Wing wrap long arms (1 and 5, 3 and 7) for 4″ using
6 rounds multicolor
6 rounds rust
6 rounds dark gold
6 rounds multicolor
6 rounds rust
6 rounds dark brown

Step 8: Measure from center of eye to end of wings. Weave should be about 8¼″ to 8½″. Short arm wrappings should measure 4¼″ to 4½″ the same way. Adjust weaving accordingly.

Step 9: To make a four-pointed star, front wrap 3 rounds of bright gold on all arms. Push each wrap towards the eye and glue in place.

Step 10: Wind the short arms (2, 4, 6 and 8) with taupe all the way to the ends, gluing as you go. These covered ends may be part of the design, or you may cover them with the wraps which follow.

Step 11: Now, with only the long arms (1, 3, 5 and 7) to weave on, back wrap 4 rounds dark brown
4 rounds taupe
4 rounds dark gold
4 rounds taupe

Step 12: Front wrap 4 rounds rust
4 rounds multicolor
4 rounds dark gold

Step 13: Back wrap 8 rounds taupe
4 rounds bright gold

Step 14: Front wrap 2 rounds rust
2 rounds dark brown
2 rounds bright gold
2 rounds dark brown
4 rounds rust

Step 15: Back wrap 8 rounds dark gold
Step 16: Add loop for hanging on Arm 5.

Step 17: Front wrap 3 rounds rust
3 rounds multicolor
4 rounds bright gold

Step 18: Back wrap multicolor for about 1½" or until wrapping reaches about 1½" from end of arms.

Step 19: Glue remaining wood and wind with multicolor.
Step 20: Add rust tassels.

Moon Shot

Materials

One 36″ dowel ⅜″ in diameter, cut into 4 lengths—
17″, 8″ and two 5½″.

Suggested yarn colors: melon, purple, yellow and
apple green (1 oz. each)

Step 1: Notch 17″ dowel in middle. Notch 8″ dowel and
glue to notch in long dowel. Turn skeleton edgewise
from the front of the cross. Notch the 17″ dowel 3″
from each end, so that the notches face you and are
90° around the 17″ dowel from the center notch.
Notch 5½″ dowels in middle and glue to end notches.

Step 2: Double weave an eye, on the middle crossed dowels, measuring 2″ square using melon yarn.

Step 3: Double weave identical eyes on the top and bottom crossed dowels with melon.

Step 4: Wind exposed wood *between* the Ojos with melon.

Step 5: Hold the skeleton as shown in the first diagram below. Consider this its front side. In pencil, number the ends of the arms following the diagram. Using purple yarn, begin to wrap the first round from Arm 1. Wrapping each arm completely, string the yarn from Arm 1 to 2 to 5 to 6, and return to Arm 1. Wrap tightly and push all the wraps toward the center Ojos to get the proper tension. Twirl the skeleton to its reverse side, and follow the directions in the second diagram.

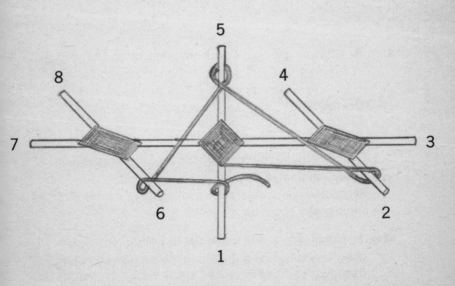

Front

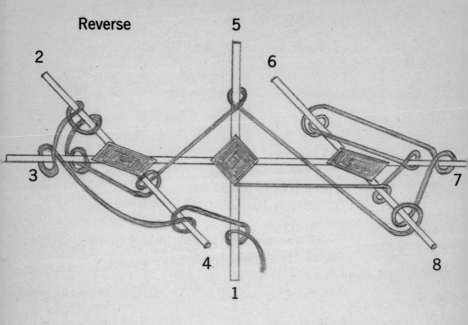

Reverse

Step 6: With the reverse side facing you, wrap the yarn from Arm 1 to 8 to 7 and to 6. Return to Arm 7, then to 8. Continue wrapping to Arm 5 to 4 to 3 and to 2. Then go back to Arm 3 to 4, and return to Arm 1.

Step 7: Twirl the skeleton to its front side and repeat entire procedure (steps 5 and 6).

Step 8: Wrap 8 rounds purple
10 rounds yellow
15 rounds green

Step 9: If you have not reached the tips of the arms, continue wrapping apple green, gluing as you go until no wood shows.

Step 10: Cover the ends of the main long arm with green. Glue.

Step 11: Attach a long piece of string or wire to the end of the long dowel and hang the Ojo as a mobile.

Note: This design is actually made by weaving a regular Ojo on the front and reverse sides of the skeleton. After the first round is strung, you can easily use it as a guide.

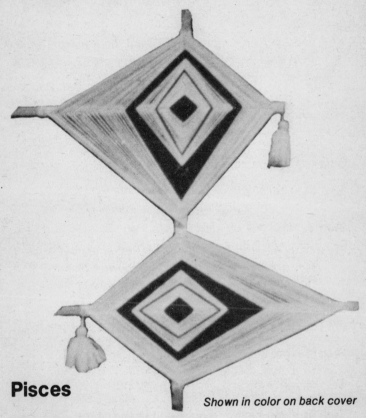

Pisces

Shown in color on back cover

Materials

Three flat sticks ¾˝ x ½˝, two 22˝ lengths and one 32˝ length.

Suggested yarn colors: turquoise, lime green and red (1 oz. each)

Step 1: Notch the 32″ stick 7¾″ from each end. Notch the two 22″ sticks 7½″ from one end. Place the 32″ stick vertically. Place the notch of one of the 22″ sticks over the upper notch in the 32″ stick with the longer end at the left. Place the notch of the other 22″ stick over the lower notch of the 32″ stick, with the longer end at the right. Glue at the notches and let dry.

Step 2: Start wrapping the kite Ojo at the top. Front wrap an eye about 2″ wide with green yarn. (All wrapping on this project is done on the front.)

Step 3: Wrap 14 rounds turquoise. Single wrap Arms 2 and 4 and wrap 2 on Arms 1 and 3 until the weaving forms a diamond approximately 6″ x 3¾″.

Step 4: Add 2 rounds of red.

Step 5: Wrap 9 rounds turquoise; single wrapping Arms 1 and 3 and giving Arms 2 and 4 wrap 3, so that the strands separate slightly.

Step 6: Next, wrap 11 rounds of green; wrapping Arms 2, 3 and 4 once, but continuing to wrap 3 on Arm 1. Then extend wrappings on Arm 1 to wrap 4 or 5 so that the strands separate about ⅛″.

Step 7: Wrap 23 rounds turquoise. Arms 1 and 3 now receive single wrap, while Arm 4 receives wrap 3 (slowly extending to wrap 4 or 5 to separate strands) and Arm 2 receives wrap 2. Overall dimension of the finished kite Ojo should be about 17″ x 13¾″. Use glue freely throughout to keep shape.

Step 8: Start wrapping lower Ojo, making an eye about 2″ wide with green yarn.

Step 9: Wrap 16 rounds turquoise; single wrap Arms 1 and 3, wrap 2 Arms 2 and 4 until diamond measures 3⅝″ x 5½″.

Step 10: Wrap 2 rounds red.

Step 11: Wrap 7 rounds turquoise; wrap 2 or 3 on Arms 1 and 3 so that strands separate slightly, single wrap Arms 2 and 4.

Step 12: Wrap 11 rounds green; wrap Arms 1 and 3 once, wrap 2 Arm 4 and wrap 3 or 4 on Arm 2 so that the strands separate ⅛″.

Step 13: Wrap 23 rounds turquoise. At first, single wrap Arms 1 and 3, then expand to wrap 2. For Arm 4, single wrap first few rounds, then wrap 2. Wrap 3 Arm 2, then expand to wrap 4 then 6 until the turquoise wrappings on this arm measures 6″. Overall measurement of the kite should be 19″ x 11½″.

Step 14: Glue and cut yarn, then work or sew loose ends into wrappings with pin or needle. Attach tassels to short right and left arms, and cut long right and left arms to point or angle if desired.